SAFETY
AND
SECURITY
IN SCHOOLS

A GUIDE TO SCHOOLS
FOR SAFETY AND SECURITY

MANOJ KUMAR

INDIA · SINGAPORE · MALAYSIA

Notion Press

No.8, 3rd Cross Street,
CIT Colony, Mylapore,
Chennai, Tamil Nadu – 600004

First Published by Notion Press 2020
Copyright © Manoj Kumar 2020
All Rights Reserved.

ISBN 978-1-63745-340-7

INDEX

PREFACE

Children spend most of their time in school, the concern of parents about the safety of school children are increasing every other day regarding their physical safety, mental health or child abuse owing to increasing incidents involving safety and wellbeing of school children.

A good education institute is one in which every student feels welcomed and cared for, where a safe and stimulating learning environment exists. To ensure safety and security of the students in schools, various circulars guidelines, notifications, government orders, manuals etc have been issued from time to time by various government agencies. Hence, all the institutions have to develop their safety procedure according to these guidelines to handle unforeseen situations and circumstances.

Also, safety at the schools is not a one time static process; it is an ongoing dynamic process involving identification of safety needs, developing prevention, response and preparedness protocols, evaluating physical facilities and providing communication and training for staff members and students.

The measures mentioned in the book, have been taken from various circulars, guidelines issued time to time by different government agencies as MHRD, NCPCR, CBSE, CISCE, Police Deptt etc for the Safety of School Students. These all have been compiled together here in a form of book for the betterment of Schools. I am sure all of you will go through the points mentioned in the book and implement them in your organization to create a safe and secure environment for our students and staff.

Manoj Kumar

SCHOOL BUILDING

1. School building needs to be certified as safe for housing the students by the local authorities.

2. Constructions should be done of 'A' Class with brick/stone masonry walls with RCC roofing.

3. Structural standards of school building and its components such as corridors, staircases, side area, quality of construction should be as per the National Building Code.

4. The Pre Primary schools/classes should be housed on the ground floor and the maximum number of floors in school building shall be restricted to three including the ground floor.

5. The school building shall be free from inflammable and toxic materials, which if necessary, should be stored away from the school building.

6. The staircases, which act as exits of escape routes, shall adhere to provisions specified in the National building Code of India to ensure quick evacuation of children.

7. The orientation of the building shall be in such a way that proper air circulation and lighting is available with open space all-round the building as far as possible.

8. Existing school buildings shall be provided with additional doors in the main entrances as well as the class rooms if required. The size of the main exit and classroom doors shall be enlarged if found inadequate.

9. School buildings have to be insured against fire and nature calamities with Group insurance of the school students and staff.

10. Kitchen and other activities involving use of fire shall be carried out in a secure and safe location away from the main school building.

11. All schools shall have water storage tanks, duly covered and protected.

12. CCTV in schools needs to be monitored and maintained regularly.

13. The steps leading to the terrace should be locked with no entry being permitted. Only authorized staff/personnel may be permitted for maintenance purposes under supervision.

14. The water tanks on the terrace must be covered, sealed and locked. Entry must be confined only to the authorized staff.

15. Building Safety or Structural Safety Certificate should be obtained by competent authority.

16. There should be ramps/elevators for the disabled persons.

17. The entire school premises should not have any kind of sharp object protruding out that can inure children.

18. All areas of the building should be well-lit and well ventilated.

19. The building should be constructed in accordance to the fire safety norms.

20. Overhead tanks, sumps should be clean on periodically basis, date of cleaning should be recorded for its review.

21. School should have proper system for disposal of waste and garbage.

22. Drains, sumps, bore wells and overhead tanks in school should be closed.

23. School building should have elevators and it should be manned at all times.

24. Maintenance of lifts must be done by a person registered with the Chief Inspectors of Lifts.

25. Drains in the school vicinity should be closed and cordoned off securely.

*****

CLASSROOM

1. The guideline issued by the Ministry of HRD, talks about class room safety.

2. The classrooms should be white washed at periodic intervals and dusted regularly to maintain the class room hygiene.

3. The windows should be secure and there should be no broken glass or fittings hanging loose.

4. Black/white board in the class room may be hung, placed in a three legged stand to keep on a chair.

5. Black/white boards are also attached to the wall of the classroom.

6. In case of loosely placed black/white board in the classroom, there is a possibility of accidents, both minor and major, to the children while moving around in the classroom.

7. While constructing school building, provision of adequate ventilators and windows in the class should be considered.

8. Class room floor should not be broken or uneven

and may need to be repaired/maintained from time to time.

9. Each class rooms should have two doors for easy evacuation; adequate openings for ventilation and lighting are some of the essential elements that need to be accommodated in the design.

10. Opening of doors of classrooms must be inside to avoid any clash in the corridors.

11. All items of furniture such as Almirahs, shelves, black boards, etc as well as any other items that may fall and cause injury to students and teachers such as ceiling fans, coolers, water tanks etc need to be secured to the walls or floor.

12. Furniture in the classrooms should be arranged in such a way that there is adequate space between rows and tables and chairs, for easy movement in the classrooms.

13. The furniture must not have any protruding nails, splinter etc. sharp edged furniture should not be a part of the school furniture.

14. Children must not carry any sharp objects in/on their possession. Random check up should be done by the teachers for it.

15. School bags should not be kept in the passage ways to avoid any injury to students while walking in corridors.

16. Classes should be under CCTV surveillance. As per the requirement one or two CCTV can be put, however, it should cover whole classroom area.

17. No corporal punishment should be initiated for the students.

18. Teacher should avoid any kind of seclusion, restraint, violence and humiliation with children.

19. Attendance should be taken in classroom on daily basis and school should share a message to all absentees in morning.

20. School should review absenteeism regularly and takes steps to ensure regular attendance.

21. Benches, desks should sturdy and should be made of wood, mould plastic. If these are of metal or any other material then should have round edges.

22. School has to maintain good condition of its building, fixtures, furniture, equipment, lavatories and play ground.

23. Children should wear their ID cards at all times.

24. ID cards should contain details as Name, Class, section, Blood Group, Bus route (if any), Parent's Name and number and Photograph of child.

25. The doors of the classrooms should have glass window so that it can be visible from outside if the doors are closed during classrooms.

*****

LABORATORY

Laboratories in school must be positioned as per the rules as mentioned below:

1. The space for free mobility for students in case of an emergency must be maintained.

2. The chemicals and instruments must be kept safely beyond the easy access of children and should be used only under supervision.

3. A first aid box must be made available in the lab.

4. There should be an exhaust facility for the gases.

5. The school team must be trained to meet any emergency in the laboratory.

6. A display board mentioning Dos and DON'Ts should be put up inside at a prominent place in the premises in local language for everyone's understanding.

7. Chemical and any hazardous materials in the school laboratory should be handled and stored as per instructions to prevent any harm to students and school staff.

8. Proper instructions should be given to all students before conducting any kind of practical as well as a written chart of safety measures should be displayed at various places in the labs.

9. Regular checkup should be done of the first aid equipment.

10. Eye washers' should be used on weekly basis just to check its working and avoid the gathering of any rust/dust etc in the water.

11. The laboratory must never be left unattended nor unsupervised. The teacher and or the laboratory assistant must conduct regular rounds to ensure maintenance of discipline in the laboratory.

12. Teachers should ensure to develop the attitude in their students toward safety while conducting practical.

13. There should be a proper record of all the equipment as well as material.

14. Designing of all science laboratories according to necessary norms and standards.

15. There should be two wide doors for unobstructed exits from the laboratory.

16. Adequate number of fire extinguishers should be placed near science laboratories.

17. Periodical checking of vulnerable points in the laboratories in relation to possibility of any mis-

happening.

18. Ensuring gas fittings in Chemistry laboratory fulfilling desired norms and standards.

19. Periodical checking of electrical fittings/insulations for replacement and repairs.

20. Timely and repeated instructions to students for careful handling of chemicals and equipment in the laboratory.

21. Safe and secure storage of all chemicals and proper labelling and upkeep of chemicals.

22. Proper safety and protection provisions such as fume hood, goggles and gloves while doing practical work.

23. Careful supervision of students while doing practical work.

24. Advance precautionary arrangements to meet any emergency situations.

25. Conduct of any additional experimental work only under supervision and with due advance permission

*****

KITCHEN

1. The kitchen cum store should be located in a clean and open place and free from filthy surroundings and should be maintain overall hygienic environment.

2. The premises should be clean, adequately lighted and ventilated and have sufficient free space for the movement.

3. Floors, ceilings and walls must be maintained in a sound condition. They should be smooth and easy to clean with no flaking paint or plaster.

4. The floor and skirted walls should be washed as per the requirement with an effective disinfectant.

5. The premises should be kept free from all insects.

6. No spraying should be done during the cooking of meal, but instead fly swats/flaps should be used to kill flies getting into the premises.

7. Windows, doors and other openings should be fitted with net or screen, as appropriate to make the premises insect free.

8. The water used in the cooking should be potable.

9. Continuously supply to potable water should be ensured in the premises.

10. In case of intermittent water supply, adequate storage arrangement for water used in the food or washing should be made.

11. Arrangement of cleaning of containers, tables, working parts of machinery etc should be done.

12. All utensils should be kept clean, washed, dried and stored at the Kitchen cum store to ensure freedom from growth of mold/fungi and infestation.

13. All utensils should be placed well away from the walls to allow proper inspection.

14. There should be efficient drainage system and there should be adequate provisions for disposal of waste.

15. Potential sources of contamination like rubbish, waste water, toilet facilities, open drains and stray animals should be kept away from kitchen.

16. Kitchen should be separate from classrooms, preferably located at a safe, but accessible distance.

17. Floors should be sloped appropriately to facilitate drainage and the drainage should flow in a direction opposite to the direction of food preparation.

18. Adequate control measures should be in place to

prevent insects and rodents from entering the area from drains.

19. Windows, doors and all other openings to outside environment should preferably be covered with wire-mesh or insect proof screen as applicable to protect the premise from flies and other insects/pets/animals.

20. Ventilation system natural and/or mechanical including air filters, exhaust fans, wherever required, should be designed and constructed so that air does not flow from contaminated areas to clean areas.

21. A display board mentioning Dos and DON'Ts should be put up inside at a prominent place in the premises in local language for everyone's understanding.

22. Properly constructed chimneys are required in the kitchen. Chimneys should not be the entry point of insects; reptile's etc.

23. Fuel (Kerosene/fuel wood/charcoal/LPG) should be stored/installed safely, so that there is no fire hazard.

24. Smokeless chulhas should be used to the extent possible.

25. The kitchen should have full visibility with sunlight or artificial light.

*****

DRINKING WATER

1. Safe and adequate drinking water should be made available to the children within the school premises.

2. Adequate number of water taps should be installed for all the students and its location should be at convenient points within the school building.

3. Safety/quality of water must be checked on regular basis by the concerned deptt.

4. Water test should be done on biannually basis through an approved lab to ensure the quality of water.

5. If possible TDS check should be done on weekly basis. It's a simple process and even a plumber can do and can maintain its record.

6. Cleaning of water coolers as well as the overhead water tanks should be done on routine basis.

7. Electrical connection of the water coolers and water dispensers should be check on daily basis.

8. All areas should have their different signage in local language.

9. There should not be any water logging in the drinking water area.

10. Signage of 'Drinking Water' should be installed at the drinking water area.

11. There should be a provision of RO/Water purifier or filter.

12. Certificate of Safe Drinking water should be obtained from the Municipal or Local Health Deptt.

13. Drinking water for children should always be taken from a safe water source.

14. The water should be collected, stored and used hygienically eliminating any chance of contamination.

15. If ground water is being used for drinking, then its source should be away from the toilet pit area.

*****

TOILETS

1. Toilets must be locates within the school premises.

2. There must be separate toilets for girls and boys.

3. Separate toilets for children, staff and support staff.

4. There must be separate toilets for the visitors.

5. Every school needs to maintain number of toilets as per the prescribed norms (as per the affiliation bye laws of the board).

6. Toilets must be kept open for the use by children.

7. Separate toilets as per the norms, must be available/accessible for children with disabilities.

8. All the toilets preferably need to have running water facility.

9. Availability of soaps etc for washing hands-should be ensured by the school.

10. All the toilets must have doors for ensuring safety and privacy of children.

11. The school needs to have clean and working method of disposing waste material, especially for girls.

12. All areas should have their different signage in local language.

13. Entrance to washrooms/toilets must be under constant CCTV surveillance.

14. It is mandatory to ensure the identification and verification of all contractual staff (Sweepers/Janitors, cleaners, maids etc) who work in the toilet area.

15. Toilets/washrooms should be adequately lit and ventilated.

16. Washrooms bowls & urinals must be cleaned and disinfected daily.

17. It should be ensured that the floors are clean, dry and non-slippery.

18. Visitors/contractual staff/bus staff should not be permitted to visit the washrooms meant for students.

19. Number of toilets/Urinals should be in good proportion to number of students and staff.

20. All disinfectants and cleaning material should be kept away from the reach of the children.

*****

PLAYGROUND

1. The school should have a playground.

2. Ground should be maintained properly.

3. The children must get the games/sports material to play.

4. The school should have a boundary wall.

5. The schools that are providing specific sports or physical activity need to provide proper facilities, trained staff and necessary equipment and materials, with respect to each of them and also need to adhere to the respective guidelines.

6. Provision of adequate medical facilities in schools is required.

7. Pots/planters in the playground or corridors should be kept in manner that does not affect smooth evacuation.

8. The playground needs to be maintained and supervised on regular basis.

9. There should be no broken pieces of equipment such as broken swing, seats or slide lying around

that might cause injury to students playing on the ground.

10. Proper drainage system of the ground should be maintained. Water should not collect under or near equipment especially under the slide and swing areas.

11. The PTI/Instructor should monitor the children using playground equipment like swings, slides, merry-go-grounds, see-saw etc.

12. All kinds of Sports courts should be under CCTV coverage.

13. At sporting events such as Football, cricket, hockey, basketball, skateboarding, boxing etc a trained physical coach must be present.

14. First aid squad with a stretcher and first aid kid must be readily available when a game is being played.

15. There should not be any underground water tank under the playground. It there is any big tank etc, then it should be permanently covered on top.

*****

BOUNDARY WALL AND GATES

1. RTE Act (2009) mandates that every school should have boundary wall/fencing.

2. Boundary wall should be of sufficient height so that no one can scale it down and should be got fixed with concertina/barbed wire.

3. Boundary wall should have 3-4 gates preferably on the walls of different sides so as to ensure free, convenient and prompt exit in emergency. However entry of outsides should be allowed only through single gate properly manned by the guards.

4. The single gate should have telephone connection so as to enable the guard to inform the police directly as well as school authorities in emergency.

5. Special surveillance and safety measures should be taken before actual entry and exit time of the school.

6. At exit time of staff and students as many as gates available be used for dispersal.

7. The main gate should remain locked after entry

of students and staff. Entry of the parents and visitors should be permitted only through small doors after verifying their identity through window during well notified schedule intervals, as such vehicles of visitors should not be allowed inside the campus.

8. The entry/exit points of the school must be constantly manned by the Security guards preferably appointed from a registered security agency after due verification. School should have full details of the documents of all the security or contract staff deputed in school.

9. A separate register or any device is to be maintained for the visitors/parents which must include name of visitor/parent address, telephone/mobile no., purpose of visit, and person to be met.

10. A good quality CCTV should be installed at the gate which can have the record of all visitors coming and going at the main gate.

11. Entry of unknown person/s must be strictly prohibited in the school, entry may only be allowed with authorized permission of the school authority.

12. Students' entry should be done only from main gate. Side gates should be avoided. If side gates are necessary, they should be under supervision and any entry or exit may be recorded in a register or device by the security who are on duty.

13. Visitor pass should be given to the visitors and singed by the person to whom the visitor has met. There should be an issue time of it and security should ensure that within the given time, visitor has come back and returned the Gate pass.

14. Every person on the premises should have a valid identity card or a visitor pass. It should be ensured that all shall wear their ID Cards.

15. Access to areas like bus area, gym, swimming pools, sports rooms/fields, canteen, toilets should be confined to persons whose presence in the area is required, and are therefore specifically authorized access to these areas; loitering in such specific areas by unauthorized personnel should be prevented to reduce chances of problems.

16. Admin/Security deptt must draw up a list of restricted areas and names of persons permitted entry, and these must be displayed on an internal notice board on the premises.

17. Parents or other visitors should not have free access across premises during school hours, and if their entry is necessitated, they must be accompanies by school authority so that their access if limited and monitored.

18. Bus drivers and conductors, whether employed by the school or contracted out, access area must be limited to just the bus area, and specific instructions must be given to them on which areas are

out of bounds for them. It is also suggestive that they should have their separate toilets away from students' toilet area.

19. Special care should be taken to ensure proper sealing and monitoring of areas which are unoccupied or used less often. Ideally these areas should be covered by the CCTV and the Vigilance officer must take a round of such areas every now and then to ensure safety is not compromised.

20. Unauthorized vendors, carts, shops and other establishments in the immediate area and boundary of schools must be removed.

21. Schools may report any such cases to the local police station to get assistance in this regard.

22. No staff should be allowed to leave school premises in between of duty time without any Gate Pass or written consent of school authorities.

23. There should be different signages for the parents and visitors regarding Parking of Vehicles, Prohibition of use of Tobacco, Prohibition of carrying Fire Arms etc at the main gate.

24. If possible, the entry and exit of all support staff and vendors should be done a separate gate.

25. All the material coming in or going out must be register at the register in Security gate and it should go out only through a gate pass issued by any School authority.

*****

SCHOOL PREMISES AND SURROUNDINGS

1. Schools should adopt extensive safety of the children in school surroundings and while a festival or celebration is being carried out in schools.

2. The school should maintain a distance from railway tracks to provide a safe environment.

3. If the school is located near any rail track, main road or any highway, then impact of such location on the school structure should be examined by the local authorities for the safety of the students.

4. The school should maintain a distance from industry or chemical factor to provide a safe environment.

5. If school located near an industry or a chemical factory producing fatal chemical products, each member including teacher, student and other staff must be made aware about different chemical product and precaution to be taken in case eventualities from the leakage of chemicals in this

area.

6. First aid and other medical systems should be in place to safeguard school students.

7. Each member of school including students must be made aware on periodical basis about the procedures to be adopted in case of any emergency.

8. No liquor/opium/bhang shop should be allowed to operate in proximity of school.

9. No school staff should be allowed to go out and gather in outer area.

10. There should be a designated waiting place for the visitors to the school.

*****

INFIRMARY

1. All schools should have a well-equipped Infirmary/Medical room it its campus.

2. A trained medical staff must be appointed on duty and be available during school hours. In case of a residential school trained medical staff must be available on campus for any emergency at all times.

3. Among other essentials, first aid kit, a stretcher, a wheel chair and an oxygen cylinder must be made available for any form of medical emergency.

4. Infirmary/sick room must be under CCTV coverage and on visitor must be permitted to visit the sick room.

5. School should have a tie up with any good and nearest hospital for any kind of emergency.

6. First aid training should be given to all teachers as well as to all support staff.

7. First aid kits should be available in the Infirmary as well as in all security gates, reception area and

Sports Deptt.

8. School has to formulate 'Emergency Response Plan' and constitute 'Emergency Response Team' and School Health Committee. Its meeting should be done on periodical basis.

9. Incident report should be made of all the incidents happen in school. Proper action should be taken on the report to avoid any future incident.

10. Regular health check ups should be done of all the students and staff.

11. School should maintain relevant medical records of all students.

12. School should have agreement with any nearest and good hospital from where medical services as well as ambulance can be taken on call basis.

13. Emergency contact number of School Medical/ Emergency team as well as ambulance and hospital should be available at all prominent areas as Security gate, School reception etc.

14. Infirmary should have emergency contact nos. of all the students as well as of all the staff.

15. There should be a health club in school under the chairmanship of the Principal of School.

*****

GYMNASIUM/SPORTS ROOM

1. The gymnasium and sports room must be accessed by children under the direct supervision of the physical instructor/games teacher.

2. The instructor must emphasize on the use of personal protective equipment required in certain games or sports activities.

3. The instructor must demonstrate how the new activities are carried out before allowing children to perform.

4. If a child is not comfortable performing an exercise/activity or feels uneasy no insistence nor coercion should be used.

5. Existing machines/equipment must be inspected on a regular basis, to ensure safety norms are in place.

6. The gymnasium & sports room must be airy, well-lit and with adequate ventilation with safe flooring.

7. A first aid kit must be readily available.

8. The gymnasium/sports facilities must be under CCTV surveillance.

9. The school playgrounds, swings, rides, sports-equipment etc should be safe and maintained regularly.

10. All safety instructions pertaining to use of play equipment to be displayed at prominently near play equipment.

11. School has to ensure active supervision by teachers/trainers of children both inside and outside the classroom.

12. Periodic maintenance certificate should be done.

13. There should be proper record of attendance of all the students who go for sports.

14. There should be security guards at all the gates of Sports room.

15. Sports room should have drinking water and toilet facility.

*****

SWIMMING POOL

1. The swimming pool area must be under constant supervision of the swimming coach/instructor when in use. No visitor/nor unauthorized entry should be permitted.

2. The instructor must inspect the pool thoroughly before and after the use of the swimming pool by the students.

3. The pool must be clean and if the bottom of the pool is not visible or unclean, all events scheduled should be cancelled.

4. Swimming should not be permitted in the diving area, when diving activities are in progress.

5. Diving in the pool must be under the strict supervision of the instructor.

6. Lifesaving buoys and ropes must be easily accessible always.

7. The instructor must not leave the pool unattended if students are using the pool.

8. All necessary life saving equipment as lifesaving

buoys, bamboo stick (5 feet and 20 feet long with rope), floats, kick boards, rope approx. 20 feet long, wire with belt should be available at all times at pool area.

9. Only a limited number of swimmers and non-swimmers must be near the pool area at any given time. School should appoint qualified coaches as well as life guards for its students.

10. There should be separate change room as well as shower place for boys and girls.

11. Special care, caution and continuous supervision in swimming pool area should be done to prevent any accident or cases of drowning.

12. Access to swimming pool should be restricted to authorized persons only.

13. Swimming Pool area should be monitored under CCTV cameras.

14. All coaches and life guards should be certified from SAI.

15. Regular check of swimming pool water should be done on regular basis.

16. No swimming pool will be constructed without prior permission of the competent authority.

17. If swimming pool is constructed in school premises, it must be constructed as per the prescribed

norms of competent authority and should also be maintained as prescribed.

18. The nearby surface of the pool area should not be slippery.

19. If the area is becoming slippery then a mat should be laid in that area to avoid any slippery situation or injury.

20. If pool is covered with walls then exhaust fans should be installed sufficiently to avoid suffocation.

*****

MEASURES TO PREVENT CHILDREN FROM DANGER OF WATER AND DROWNING

1. The wells and ponds if exists in the campus are to be provided with protective wall and iron grills covering the well and the movements of the students should be restricted towards it.

2. Children should not be allowed to go towards the nearby river, canals, ponds and railway tracks and to take bath using water from the overhead tanks by climbing on the terrace.

3. Fencing should be provided to the steps of overhead tank to avoid children climbing over head tank.

4. Movements of children are to be strictly watched through formation of groups by school authorities.

5. Children should not be permitted to go outside the school premises during the school hours.

6. The presence of the students in the School campus at all times should be strictly enforced.

7. Underground water tanks must be covered at all times.

8. There should not be any open water tank in school premises.

9. If there is any tank etc on account of any specific reason and there should be a security person deputed there and entry of students should be restricted.

10. There should be signages in all local languages as well as in English for the students and staff for all water body areas.

*****

EDUCATIONAL TRIPS AND TOURS

1. If the school is organizing any educational trip, picnic or excursion, the school becomes the solely responsible for the safety and security of students.

2. The school should inform parent about the details of the trip and should take written consent from parent for the trip. No child/staff should be sent on trip without any written consent of the parents/guardian.

3. The school must obtain all details and information required in advance of the place of visit.

4. If visiting any sea coast/hill area, then written information should be taken before the trip from the concerned metrological deptt.

5. Teachers should take the attendance of students at various intervals to update the presence of absence of students going on the trip.

6. A medical staff should also accompany the trip with first aid medical kit.

7. Insurance should be done of all the staff and students going on the tour.

8. If going through road transport, then all relevant papers of the vehicles and its staff should be checked prior to boarding the vehicle.

9. Any student going for river rafting must be a good swimmer. Students must opt for these activities only with the prior permission of the parent and teacher and should perform under the supervision of an expert.

10. All necessary instructions should be given to students in terms of the required equipment i.e. camping equipment, dress, water bottles, food items etc required for the trip/excursion.

*****

CCTVS IN SCHOOLS

1. All schools must have adequate CCTVs in the school premises.

2. Cameras must cover all critical areas of the premises.

3. All specific areas as Entry and Exit of School, all corridors, staircase, library, infirmary, auditorium, inside elevators, dining halls, sports rooms, labs, entrances to classrooms, entrance to toilets, sports fields, swimming pools, areas where buses assembles, entry and exit points of school building.

4. Any point on the outer perimeter/wall which is vulnerable, and which could show footage of persons attempting to gain entry to the premises, specially covering persons outside the main entrance.

5. All kinds of plants in school as RO, Water Softener, STP, Transformer, Electric Panels, Electric Room, Fire Pump Room, Swimming Pool Pump Room etc Should have CCTV Coverage.

6. Entrance of all toilets must be under CCTV coverage. No CCTV should be installed inside any of

toilet.

7. All cameras must have point, tilt and zoom capability and the recording capacity of the footage should be at least 45 days.

8. Regular check up should be done of all person and a dedicated staff should be deputed for the CCTVs.

9. All vehicles entering and leaving the premises should be caught on camera with at least a 50 meter range with a clean image of the vehicle number.

10. A control panel must be set up with screens visible in a public place such as reception where in addition to the designed viewer, viewing is possible by any passerby including responsible persons such as teachers, the Security I/c, Safety Officer, Vigilance Officer etc.

11. All CCTV equipment must be maintained regularly and it must be ensured that once installed, the footage is viewed and the equipment used to bring in a strong control.

12. A written record of daily checkup should be made of all the CCTVs working in school.

13. All vigilance and monitoring mechanisms in the school infrastructures should be installed as per the directions of appropriate regulating authority.

14. In case of residential schools, the entire campus should be monitored through CCTV.

15. A vigilance office should be deputed in school and he or she should monitor children through CCTV Room to ensure safety of children by exercising caution and preventing any harm from being caused to them.

*****

SAFETY IN SCHOOL TRANSPORTS

Transport is also an important area that needs supervision and specific measure.

CBSE has also specifically issued a circular towards children's safety in school transport based on the Hon'ble Supreme Court guidelines.

1. Exterior of the Bus

    a. All the buses must be painted with uniform colour preferably yellow with the name of the school written prominently on both sides of the bus so that these can be identified easily.

    b. The word 'School Bus' must be written on the back and front of the bus if it is hired bus, "On School Duty" should be clearly indicated.

    c. Telephone numbers of the school and/ or telephone numbers of any contact person shall also be written prominently in a prominent place in each school bus so that in case of necessity the public can inform the school authority/police or other authorities.

d. Buses should not have curtains or dark films. There should have internal white lighting and activities in the bus should be visible from the outside.

e. Buses should have a valid certificate of fitness, pollution and insurance.

f. Buses should have horizontal grills on the windows, first aid box, fire extinguisher, speed governor and cctv.

2. Manpower in the Bus

a. Police verification of the staff of the bus should be done before their appointment.

b. There must be qualified attendant, preferably female in the Bus to attend the children.

c. Each school should designate one Transport Manager/Coordinator who will ensure the safety of the school children.

d. The provision shall also be made by the school authorities for travelling of at least one teacher in each school bus, keeping in view the safety of the school students all throughout the journey and no outsider except the conductor or the said authorized teacher or one person authorized by the guardians shall be allowed to board school bus.

e. Medical check up regarding the physical fitness of the driver including the eye testing shall be made every year.

f. Every bus should have one female teacher and one female helper/didi present on the route. Therefore the presence of an adult female is essential before the first student boards in the bus at the start of the journey and also till the last student gets off at the end of the journey. Exception may be made only if the first/last student is a male students aged 14 or above.

g. Routing should be accordingly planned so that the first and last child is not a female; also it a must to have the didi/teacher present so that the first and the last child, even if male, is not left alone with bus driver/conductor, unless the child is a male students aged 14 years of above.

h. At the time the bus begins to move from the spot both on the school ground as well as at every stop thereafter, the conductor using a whistle shall be present on the ground to check that clear access is available to move, or particularly to reverse, with no children/others in the way, and indicate with a series of short whistles to proceed, or a long whistle as a caution to stop immediately.

3. Facilities in the Bus

    a.   Bus should have a First Aid Box

    b.   To keep the school bags safely, there should be a space fitted under the seats or as convenient.

    c.   The buses should be fitted with alarm bell/siren so that in case of emergency everyone can be alerted.

4. Permits

    a.   The driver should have valid license and at least 5 years of experience of driving heavy vehicles.

    b.   A driver who has been challenged more than twice in a year for offences like red light jumping, violation of lane discipline or allowing unauthorized person to drive cannot be employed.

    c.   Periodical fitness certificate regarding roadworthiness of the vehicle should have to be obtained.

d. Any school authority and/or driver found to have violated the provision of the Motor Vehicles Act, 1988 and the rules framed there under as well as of the directions must be penalized.

e. Buses should have painted on it valid telephone numbers and mail IDs of the bus Incharge/school authority for feedback in case of improper driving; it should be updated in case of change of number. This information must be displayed even if the bus is a contract bus.

f. Parents should be informed of the telephone number and mail id of the bus I/c to whom such feedback can directed.

g. The person who made the complaint must be informed of the action taken based on the complaint within three days.

h. Complaints must be reviewed by the Head of Admin on a monthly basis. A record of such complaints must be maintained.

i. The school must have a system by which the parents should be in a position to remain connected with the school bus in case of emergency or delay.

5. Arrangements in the Schools

a. All the affiliated schools will make safe arrangement for boarding and de-boarding of school children from the school bus.

b. The school authority shall ensure that the doors of the buses remain shut while in running condition.

c. They will ensure that buses halt only at bus stops designated for the purpose and within the marked area.

d. Refresher course for driver training so as to find tune and increase the proficiency of the driver shall be given to the drivers of the school buses periodically i.e. at least twice in a year.

e. No person shall be allowed to drive the school bus in drunken condition. Regular check shall be undertaken by the school authorities and in case of any doubt in that regard such drivers must be subjected to medical test immediately and proper action including the action for cancellation of the license have to be taken.

f. All drivers of the school buses have to be dressed in a distinctive uniform with their names inscribed in it.

g. In every school bus there shall be another qualified person to keep attending children travelling in such buses, as conductor, who have to be, dressed in distinctive uniform with their names inscribed in it.

h. The school authority must provide one set of mobile phone in each school bus so that in case of emergency the bus can be contacted or he driver/conductor can contact the police or State authority as well as the school authority.

i. The authority shall ensure that the school buses are not permitted to overtake any other four wheelers while carrying the school children in the bus.

j. The school authority should ensure that the students maintain discipline when boarding and disembarking the bus so that no children get hurt.

k. Effort should be made by the school to make necessary arrangement for parking the school bus inside the school campus at least at the time of boarding and disembarking. In case it is not possible to park such vehicle inside the school campus the buses must be parked in such a way so that it does not create any traffic problem for other vehicles.

l. The school should encourage its children to conduct programmes through play, exhibition etc during Road Safety Week to create an awareness in public.

m. Periodic feedback from students using school Transport facility with regards to driver/conductor be taken and records are to be maintained.

n. The bus incharge must check and ascertain that every bus has been emptied and no child has remained in the bus.

o. In case a child who usually travels by bus is being picked up by the parent for some reason, this must be done only after due procedure of request for special depart-ment from the parent to the class teacher and a specific gate pass signed by the Bus incharge. The gate pass is to be given at the gate when the parent leaves with the child.

p. The bus driver should ensure that the doors of the bus are closed before the bus moves, children are seated, and no child is directly in front of the doors even when closed.

q. When the children get off at their bus stop near their homes, it is important that they are not left alone on the road but must be handed over only to the parent/maid or authorized representative upon showing the identity card in their custody.

r. In case the parent/guardian has not reached to pick up a child of lass 5 or below, under no circumstance should the child be left on the road. In the event there is another known parent in the same locality willing to take responsibility, this may be permitted as an exception after the teacher confirms this with the parents of the child telephonically.

s. If there is no one else to pick up the child, the child may not be permitted to alight, and the teacher in the bus will coordinate with the parent for getting off at the next convenient stop.

t. The attended in the bus shall inform the Bus Incharge about the completion of the route.

u. The driver should take care that the child does not cross the road, whenever this is feasible.

v. Under no circumstances the child be made to get out of the bus in the middle of the road forcing him/her to walk through moving traffic.

w. After the route when buses are parked,

Transport Incharge/Security Incharge in addition to Drivers and Conductors shall ensure that no child is left in bus. A through checkup should be done in morning after route as well as in evening. Also the items left by students should be submitted immediately to the Security or lost and found.

*****

FIRE SAFETY MANAGEMENT

1. Every school must have a fire safety certificate which must be validated periodically by the concerned authority.

2. School must have firefighting systems in place to meet any emergency, including the alarm system or smoke detection system.

3. With the help of firefighting agencies mock drill and training must be carried out in each school on periodical basis.

4. Trained management team should be available in the school for initial fire hazard management.

5. The school must put on display the Fire Safety and Evacuation Plan to be followed in case of emergency.

6. All the firefighting equipment should be checked on a regular period and proper written record should be maintained on daily basis.

7. All areas should have their different signage in lo-

cal language.

8. Open areas including corridors and evacuation routes including staircases and ramps should be kept free from any hurdles and barriers so that evacuation is smooth evacuation.

9. All the fire extinguishers must be regularly maintained, besides adequate standby sand and water supplies.

10. School building should be constructed in accordance to applicable fire safety norms.

11. Emergency contact numbers and list of persons to be contacted should be displayed at various places in school, especially at Security Gates as well as in reception area.

12. There should be fire alarm in school at various places and it should be checked time to time.

13. Schools should get the fire certificate renewed time to time after inspection by the concerned authorities.

14. Building above the height of 15m has to meet the provisions laid down under Fire Safety.

15. The Fire cylinders which are about to expire should be used for demonstration as well as for training to all support staff.

*****

ELECTRICAL SYSTEM AND SAFETY

1. All the electrical systems in school must be checked periodically.

2. Ensured limited access to the area of electrical installation only to those who are required.

3. The electric wiring and points are to be kept in order. In case of any uncovered live wires find, the wiring must be changed and electricity disconnected till such defects are set right.

4. The electrical distribution boxes should be locked and the keys should be kept only under the custody of electrician or the person incharge.

5. Immediate necessary measures should be taken to repair the loose wiring/connections.

6. In case of any such need electric gadgets should be handled by responsible employee of the school.

7. In few cases trees are placed just below the electric line whenever the branches grow it touches the LT line and sparks dangerously. It should be

checked regularly and branches should be dressed off in such a way that it will not touch to the electric wire any time.

8. Students should be warned not to touch electric poles.

9. All areas have their different signage in local language.

10. There should not be loose electrical wires, broken switches/sockets in the classrooms or in campus. Fans and tube lights must be fixed properly and checked routinely.

11. All electrical wiring should be concealed or insulated.

12. No high tension lines should run inside or over the school, and if they do run inside or over the school request to change such placement can be made to the relevant state authorities.

13. School has to comply with the norms of electric deptt while placing Gen sets, Transformers etc in school campus.

14. NOC of electric equipment as Transformer, DG Set etc should be obtained from concerned authority and its renewal should be done time to time.

15. The transformer, Generator (if any) should be located at the safe area, well maintained and kept

under lock.

16. Entries of students should be restricted in the electricity, DG and Transformer area.

17. Control Panels (for electricity, meter etc) must be at ground floor or upper basement area and must be located on the outer periphery of the building. It should be approved by the concerned officer of the State Electricity Board.

18. Storage of Diesel for Generators should be away from the Electricity area.

19. Big generators being installed in the campus should be sound proof to avoid any disturbance to students and staff in their routine work.

20. Electrical safety certificate should be obtained from the concerned electric deptt.

*****

EARTHQUAKE MANAGEMENT

As per the specifications of National Disaster Management Authority (NDMA), school should prepare themselves to face such calamities and should take following steps –

1. Necessary steps must be taken during construction of the building for earthquake safety.

2. If required, school must modify structure in consultation with local authority.

3. A trained disaster management group should be available for initial response.

4. School must maintain a contact with the local disaster management authorities for the regular training of students and staff.

5. An Evacuation Plan of the school should be made ready and it should be shared with all students and staff.

6. Training of evacuation should be done on a regular period of time.

7. The school must put on display the Earth Quake Management & Evacuation Plan to be followed in case of emergency.

8. Two to three assembly area should be identified as a safe place to gather during such activity.

9. Proper signage should be put at the respective assembly areas.

10. School has to plan and formulate a "Disaster Response Plan" and constitute an 'Emergency Response Team'.

11. It should consists with the members of Administration, teachers and senior students who are oriented to carry out an evacuation drill.

12. The details of the team should be introduced to all students and staff. Senior Students should also be the part of the team.

13. Emergency contact number of the team should be displayed at various prominent places in the school.

14. Proper Standard Operating Procedure (SOP) should be made for dealing with any emergency.

15. School should follow guidelines issued by the Ministry for Disaster Management for School safety.

*****

SAFETY FROM CONSTRUCTIONAL HAZARDS

1. School must obtain necessary permission from the local authorities for the construction and repair work.

2. The construction must be planned during the lean time of students' presence in the school.

3. Barricades and signboards must be installed in the construction area prohibiting the movements of the students.

4. Water storage sources for such constructions must be covered to prevent small children from any possible mishap.

5. Entry area of the labours should be separate from the entry area of students.

6. No labour should be allowed in any case in the area where children study, play or do their activities.

7. There should be a proper documentation of the labour working in school and they should be issued ID card with some different colour so that they can be easily recognized.

8. Construction work should be done in the guidelines of any trained supervisor or civil engineer.

9. Construction area should be barricaded and no child should be allowed in that site.

10. Proper guards should be deputed to avoid the entries of any unnecessary persons in the under construction sites.

*****

SAFETY DURING CELEBRATION OF FESTIVALS.

1. Adequate precautions should be taken with regard to the movement of children inside the campus during celebration of festival days in schools.

2. Teachers should be put on duty to organize the activities as per schedule plan.

3. Special care should be taken to see that children do not move, around the hazardous and dangerous points.

4. No procession should be allowed to move from out of the school campus on the eve of such celebrations.

5. Wherever the immersion of idol etc is involved during festival, the Principal should ensure that the image/idols are handed over by the students in the Campus itself and the Principal shall arrange immersion through outsider/security personnel.

6. All staff members are required to be properly briefed before commencement of any programme regarding safety of children.

7. Strict vigil to be done on Senior Students in campus.

8. All unnecessary rooms should be locked during any event or celebration in school.

9. There should be proper IDs or Passes for the visitors.

10. Students should be divided in groups and Teachers should be made incharges of it accordingly so that eye on students' activities can be done by their teachers easily.

*****

SAFETY RELATING TO STAFF

1. No candidate with a criminal record of sexual and/or physical violence may be recruited or any position within a school/institution.

2. A police verification should be done of all the employees working in school.

3. Apart from the verification of antecedents, it is recommended that the interview panel consists of the School Counselor who is able to provide a psychological profile of the person being considered for the employment.

4. Till such time references are being verified, the services of the person may be utilized but only on probation.

5. All selected candidates must provide a signed affidavit to the institution that they have not been accused of offences under POSCO (Protection of Children from Sexual Offences) Act 2012 and JJ (Juvenile Justice, Care & Protection of Children) Act 2000

6. At the time of being given the appointment letter, all candidates should be shared the details of

School's Child Protection Policy document and code of conduct, and will be required to sign it.

7. All support staff including the school nurse must be interviewed by a counsellor and recruited only after a due back ground check and police verification, especially those who have access to toilets, medical rooms, such as cleaners, helpers (Didis), nurse etc.

8. All support staff including drivers, conducts, peon,security, cleaners etc whether appointed on school roll or contract or through agency must be verified through police verification. A copy of police verification alongwith photographs, documents of their home town, two references from home town and two references from the present address, Medical fitness certificates must be maintained in school record.

9. In case of any employee or other person employed at a school being accused of an offense under POCSO, the JJ Act or any other sexual crime or violence, the person so accused should be removed from active duty with immediate effect pending enquiry as per the due process established by law.

10. A proper code of conduct should be made by school and it should be shared with all staff at the time of appointment.

*****

SAFETY FROM CONTAGIOUS DISEASES/ COVID

1. Maintain vigilance for increasing absenteeism due to respiratory, gastrointestinal or other communicable illnesses.

2. Report any increases in absenteeism rates or suspected outbreaks to your local health department immediately.

3. Collaborate with your local health department. They are there to help with outbreak investigations and can provide education about prevention and control of communicable diseases in schools.

4. Understand the basic information about diseases, including its symptoms, complications, how it is transmitted and how to prevent transmission.

5. Teachers and medical staff in school should have their eye upon such cases and recognize the symptoms of diseases.

6. If any case is found then parents or guardian should be informed and advise from Sr. Medical Officer should be taken for it.

7. Avoid students and staff with symptoms of diseases coming to school or office till they are medical proved to come.

8. Promote and demonstrate regular hand washing and positive hygiene behaviors and monitor their uptake.

9. Ensure adequate, clean and separate toilets for boys and girls.

10. Ensure soap and safe water is available at age-appropriate hand washing stations.

11. Clean and disinfect school building, classrooms and especially water and sanitation facilities at least once a day, particularly surfaces that are touched by many people (railing, lunch tables, sports equipment, door and window handles, toys, teaching and learning aids etc).

12. Increase air flow and ventilation where climate allows (open windows, use air conditioning where available etc).

13. Post signs encouraging good hand and respiratory hygiene practices.

14. Ensure trash is removed daily and disposed of safely.

15. Help the affected child or staff to cope with stress.

16. Help children to understand the basic concepts of disease presentation and control.

17. During the period of any contagious diseases, students and staff should be encouraged to wear mask in a proper manner.

18. Instead of keeping children out of school, teach them good hand and respiratory hygiene practices in school.

19. Stay home when ill: Strongly suggest that ill children and staff stay home when ill. Avoid close contact with others during the infectious period. Consult with local public health for guidance.

20. Education: Be informed about signs, symptoms and prevention of diseases. Share information with students and parents. Learning how diseases are transmitted can help to actively prevent the spread of disease.

21. Disinfect surfaces: Clean and disinfect surfaces or objects. Focus especially on frequently touched surfaces at home, work and school.

22. Vaccinate: Be sure to check immunization status of children for those diseases that can be prevented with vaccines.

23. Seek care: Visit your health care provider when ill to get diagnosed and treated properly. Keep a

supply of alcohol-based hand sanitizer and sanitizing wipes.

24. Provide reminders in daily announcements about preventing the spread of germs and illnesses.

25. Adopt healthy practices, such as safe handling of food and the use of standard precautions when handling body fluids and excretions.

*****

BARRIER FREE ACCESS FOR CHILDREN WITH DISABILITIES

1. Ramps must be constructed to provide access to the following places:

    ➢ Entry to the school

    ➢ Classrooms

    ➢ Toilets

    ➢ Playground

    ➢ Library

    ➢ Canteen

    ➢ Auditorium/Hall

    ➢ Floor to floor

2. Railings need to be provided on the both sides of ramp.

3. The school needs to make provision for children (children with visual impairment and low vision)

to move around in the school safely and inde-
pendently.

4. The school should make provision to provide a
school map in Braille indicating all the facilities
including classrooms, common rooms, library,
toilets etc that may be suitably placed at the main
gate of the school or at any other suitable place.

5. All the classrooms should have the signage in
Braille for children with visual impairment.

6. An emergency and evacuation plan of the school
should also be in Braille.

7. Also, it is important to:

   a. List of all children with disabilities in
   school must be prepared.

   b. Training must be provided to teachers and
   other staffs to understand their limitations
   and procedures to help them in the event
   of any emergency.

   c. There should be a designated official in
   the school who is entrusted with the ex-
   clusive responsibility of their needs in any
   emergency.

8. Strict discipline and to check the unauthorized
absence of the students from the School is to be
given paramount importance.

9. The root cause for such behavior of the child

must be ascertained, parents should be informed accordingly and corrective steps should be taken.

10. For certain ritual and functions which are observed in the school, necessary precautions and arrangements to be made in advance.

11. Children should not be permitted to go on rallies for immersion of idols in tanks, ponds and wells etc.

12. No procession should be allowed to move from school out of the campus in the eve of any religious celebrations.

13. School environment should be disability friendly with infrastructure facilities to suit students with special needs and as provided in the department guidelines and MHRD standards.

14. School facilities like classrooms, play areas, toilets, drinking water, labs and all rooms for children should be accessible for differently abled children.

15. Maintenance of all aids and assistive devices that are provided by the school for children with special needs.

*****

SAFETY AUDITS AND TRAININGS

1. School should have routine Audits of School Safety, School building, Water and Sanitation, Electrical Fittings, School Transport, CCTVs, Fire Fighting equipment and its NOCs should be obtained from the concerned authorities time to time.

2. Schools should have all the clearances and certificates required for verifying the safety and fitness for the school building.

3. All teaching, non-teaching, contractual and other staff should be sensitized on the Child Protection Policy & guidelines and child related legislation such as POCSO.

4. All parents and students should be made aware of the School Child Protection and Policy/Guidelines and reporting mechanisms.

5. Staff should be made to read and sign the policies framed in the school. Parents should also be involved in the policies whichever are required for them.

*****

AWARENESS SESSIONS

It is important to create an awareness among all sections of personnel associated with a school, namely children, staff and parents about the risks involved with regard to child safety and simple preventive measures that can be taken to reduce these risks. Hence awareness sessions should be done on routine basis for the students as below -

1. Awareness of bullying, other form of physical or sexual abuse.

2. Good touch, Bad touch

3. Safety from Strangers'

4. Yell, Run and Tell

5. Dangers from Known people

6. Internet Safety

7. Breaking the Code of Silence

8. Road safety

9. Self defense

10. Legal literacy

11. E-waste

12. Water Conservation

13. Save Electricity

14. Plantation/Save Trees

15. Health & Hygiene

16. Adolescent education

17. Gender sensitization

18. Human values

19. Respect to our Social Helpers

20. Pollution

21. Special needs training.

22. Life skill training

23. Social, Emotional & Sexual Safety Training

24. Fire Safety Training.

25. First aid training.

*****

FEEDBACK MECHANISMS

All schools should put in a place a serious of various levels of checks and mechanisms by which any untoward incident that puts the safety of children at risk must be prevented. To provide multiple feedback channels to suit the inclinations of every child, the following feedback mechanisms are suggested for every school:

1. Concept of Buddy – Every child must be encouraged to have an avenue by which any single case of abuse gets reported. Hence assigning a buddy (friend) from an older class is one good way to doing this.

2. Counselor- every school must have a qualified counselor who should have her connect with the children. Counsellor should also have eye upon the behavior of students as well as support staff also.

3. Helpline – Each school should have a helpline which details should be shared with all students and staff.

4. Complaint Box – There should be a complaint box in each school so that children can share their problems if any. To make the students feel comfort, it should be placed in an area which does not come under CCTV.

5. Suggestion Box- There should be suggestion boxes for students in school. These boxes should be opened on routine basis and action should be taken on the feedbacks received.

*****

SOPs/MANUAL IN SCHOOLS

All schools should have their own SOPs/Manuals of different heads as following to ensure smooth process:

1. SOP of Admission
2. SOP of Security
3. SOP of Transport
4. SOP of Cleaning & Maintenance
5. SOP of Disaster Management
6. SOP of Purchase
7. Staff Rules Booklet/HR Manual
8. SOP of Event
9. SOP of Stock & Inventory

*****

COMMITTEES IN SCHOOLS

All schools should form following essential committees (as per the directives of the Govt.) except other mandatory committees as instructed by their Board for its students and staff. Regular meetings should be done of these committees as well as its minutes should be recorded. Also, students and staff should be made aware of these committees and its purposes.

1. School Management Committee

2. Staff Selection Committee

3. Parent – Teacher Coordination Committee

4. POCSO (Protection of Children from Sexual Offence) Act 2012.

5. The Sexual Harassments of Women at Workplace (Prevention, Prohibition and Redressal) Act, 2013.

6. Disaster Management Committee

7. School Transport Committee

8. Students' Discipline Committee

9. Students' Forum

10. Different Clubs

11. Emergency Response Team

12. Any other committee as per the direction of Central as well as State Government rules.

*****

MECHANISM FOR REPORTING A CASE OF ABUSE

In case a child feels the need to report discomfort of any sort against any process or person that makes him/her feel threatened, the child must be made aware of the ways to approach the school management, to bring such cases to light.

1. Reporting could be through the class teacher, any other teacher, counsellor, buddy, helpline, complaint box or through any other responsible adult whom the child trusts in the situation.

2. All school notice boards shall display the Safe Zone Poster so that children are aware of how to route their feedback in case of any problem.

3. Any feedback that is of preventive nature must be immediately brought to the attention of the relevant person and if necessary, a special meeting of the School Committee should be called.

4. Remedial measures must be taken to prevent re-

currence of the problem within three working days.

5. A log of such feedback received and action taken must be maintained which is subject to inspection.

6. Such log must not compromise confidentially of the child, so depending on the sensitivity of the situation, if may be decided to withhold the name of the child in the log, or just list the roll number rather than name, which will be decided by the school counsellor and Principal.

7. If the abuse happened at the school or during travel, this must be immediately brought to the attention of the School Counselor, Principal and Parents of the child.

8. If the abuse happened at home, then this must be discussed by the School Counselor and at least one other School Committee member to decide which is the best way to protect the child, and accordingly parent(s) not involved in the abuse may be informed.

9. There should be confidentially at all levels of inspection, vigilance of case.

10. No facts should be hide from the parent of the child.

11. To see the seriousness of the case, it should be reported to the local police station with the consultation of parent.

12. As per the seriousness of the case, help of child safety expert can be taken to resolve the case.

13. The school must initiate investigations within the first 24 hours, whenever or not it is a working day if it is severe case where there is injury to the child requiring medical attention; if it is a routine case, then investigations must begin by the first working day.

14. Head of School should ensure that no corporal punishment should be initiated of any kind with any of the child in school.

15. There should be transparency in all investigations and school should not try to hide any facts of child abuse case with parent or with any investigation agency.

*****

Made in the USA
Monee, IL
02 August 2023